Ask Yourself

www.mascotbooks.com

Ask Yourself: Inspiring Questions for Health, Happiness, and Self-Discovery

Cover image from vecteezy.com.

For more information, please contact:
Mascot Books, an imprint of Amplify Publishing Group
620 Herndon Parkway #320
Herndon, VA 20170
info@mascotbooks.com

Library of Congress Control Number: 2021923301

CPSIA Code: PREG0522A
ISBN-13: 978-1-63755-228-5

Printed in China

Ask Yourself

Inspiring Questions for Health, Happiness, and Self-Discovery

MIKE PARKER

Introduction

You are about to embark on the most inspiring journey of self-discovery you have ever been on. This journal is sure to help you create more happiness, boost your well-being, and spark positive emotions. When you *Ask Yourself* these inspiring questions, you will be astonished by where your answers will take you.

Here is the truth about happiness: it comes, and it goes, and it's very fickle. No matter how tight your grip on it is at any given moment, it will still fade away. Here is another truth about happiness: the best news about it is that you are in control of a very large portion of your happiness. Your focus, mindset, choices, and actions—all things you are in control of—will impact your daily and long-term happiness more than anything else. As you journey through this inspiring journal that is specifically designed to take you on the most amazing trip through your happiest of memories, best experiences, and most wonderful people in your life, you will undoubtedly be reminded of why you have so much to be happy about today and into the future.

This journal is not full of a bunch of unrealistic hypothetical questions; it's full of uplifting questions that will lead to inspiring answers. These questions will bring the best, most inspiring times of your life to the forefront of your mind so that you can be reminded and motivated by who you are, what you have, and what you can do in the future.

Acknowledgments

This book is the result of a long-standing belief that everyone has inspiring stories, joyful memories, and heroic people in their lives. Often the speed of life can lead to those wonderful times and people being nothing more than a small dot in the rearview mirror of our day. When you are able to keep those amazing moments and people in the forefront of your mind, they are able to inspire and empower you over and over again.

I am deeply thankful to more people than this book can possibly hold. My heart is full of gratitude toward my many loyal and loving family members, friends, and coworkers. There is no way I can assign a hierarchy or name everyone, but here are just a few of the many.

To my wife, Brenda, you are the most supportive, kind, and loving human being I have ever been blessed to know. You have been such a huge part of nearly every achievement in my life for the past thirty years. No one has ever encouraged and believed in me more than you have. Your ability to be the most gifted elementary principal to your staff and students, the most amazing mother to our daughter, and the greatest wife and teammate I could ever hope to have never ceases to amaze me. I love you, no matter what, forever and always.

To my precious daughter, Sofia, you are the light of my life. You have brought me more smiles, laughter, joy, and love than I ever thought was possible. God has blessed you with everything you need to be the world changer you are inspired to be. Every day is brighter and better with you in it. Never forget why I love you so much: simply because you are Sofia Rose Parker.

To my daughter, Bailey, you are never far from my thoughts, and you will never be forgotten. I pray someday I get to see you with open eyes.

To my hero and dad, Jerry, thank you for showing me and teaching me what hard work really is. Words cannot explain how valuable of a lesson that has been throughout my life. I aspire to achieve a fraction of what you have throughout your life. The astonishing impact you have had on your hometown and county as an elected official for over fifty years is the story that inspires me every day of my life.

To my mom, Mamie, I am eternally grateful for more things than this short section can hold, but your commitment to making sure I was in church has helped me become the man that I am more than anything in my life. You are without question the toughest woman I know, and it brings joy to my heart to see that trait and many more in Sofia with each passing day.

To my sisters, Lisa, Laura, and Marty, there is no brother more grateful for his sisters than I am. Though we may live miles apart, you are never separated from my heart. I cherish every second I get to spend with you, and always will.

To my mother-in-law, Jean, and my father-in-law, Pat, thank you for your endless support. It has had such a positive impact on my life and our family. You both have been an outstanding example of the good that can be found within normal, hardworking people.

To my church family at Life House Church, nothing governs who I am more than my desire to live a life pleasing to God, and I am so blessed to have the loving support and encouragement from all of you as I stumble and fall and get back up again and again.

To all of my many assistant coaches over the last twenty-five years, you have been such a big part of the unprecedented success we have been able to enjoy together. Not only have you had such a positive influence on the lives of so many young people, but you all have impacted my life as well. Though we have enjoyed way more of the thrills of victory than of the agonies of defeat, I cherish the memories of both. Thank you for your relentless commitment to succeeding at the highest level with the greatest of integrity and kindness.

To my athletes, though there is no way I can begin to list the over twenty-five years of athletes I have been so blessed to coach, please know you have left a meaningful impact on my life. With some I have forged closer post-coaching relationships than with others, but know that few things bring a bigger smile to my face than seeing one of my former athletes.

To all of my motivational speaking clients, as well as my many Life and Success Coaching clients, thank you for trusting in me to inspire, empower, and educate you and the many attendees of your events. I am driven by my passion to help everyone live a motivated and inspired life and am deeply grateful for the opportunities you have given me to do just that.

To the tens of thousands of motivational speech attendees, your stories, letters, emails, and calls are so moving and meaningful to me. Your enthusiasm, engagement, and involvement has always been a source of inspiration for me at every single speech I have ever delivered.

To all the amazing people at Iowa City West High, Where Excellence is a Tradition. West High has been part of my nearly every day for the past twenty-five years. You have given me the opportunity to work with, work for, and get to know so many of the best of the best.

To everyone that I have worked with at Mascot Books, especially Jess and Jenna, who found me, convinced me, educated me, and believed in me and this book from day one.

Author's Note

Why Remind Yourself?

Keeping a journal of the positive and uplifting experiences and people you have enjoyed throughout your life will help you appreciate how meaningful and useful they are. It will also easily allow you to savor, relive, and delight in those memories and people again and again.

"Memories last forever if you write them down."
Mike Parker

How To Use This Journal

I have created *Ask Yourself* to be inspiring, uplifting, and fun. Your answers to these questions will take you on the most inspiring journey of self-discovery. There are no rules here, no order to follow; start wherever you want. Flip through until you find the question that best hits home with you on that day. The beautifully designed interior provides space on each page to write down your answers, thoughts, and reflections. There will be questions you'll want to take your time on, savoring a memory with lots of details and emotion. There will be some questions that might just require a few sentences, and others that you will want to leave for another day. There is no rush. There are inspiring questions that will fit within those times in our life when we have at best a minute or two to spare, and there are questions for those times when you want to relax, enjoy, and savor those emotional memories that take you to the best moments in your life.

Some questions are about today; others are about this week, month, or year; and some are about your life as a whole. Some questions will inspire you to take action to find the answer to the question. You can use this journal as part of your personal relaxation time. It will help you identify positive thoughts and recognize positive triggers in your life.

Ask Yourself is meant to help you enjoy life more abundantly by finding inspiration in the best of times and in people from your past, present, and future. This journal will guide you into a deep dive of your own personal memories, which will allow you to savor each and every one of them better than you ever have before.

Ask Yourself will help you create a list of the most meaningful, inspiring, and loved memories, thoughts, and people in your life. When you're done, keep it close by, carry it around—it will serve as a reminder of the best times in your life and as a source of inspiration. Maybe pick a day each month to read though some of your answers, and be whisked away to those moments, enjoying the memories that have made you the unique person you are.

As you work your way through this inspiring journal, be ready to laugh, smile from ear to ear, enjoy positive emotions, relive your many accomplishments, and be reminded of your healthiest relationships. There is no better tool to help you with personal reflection on the most inspiring times of your life. Have fun, *Ask Yourself*, remind yourself, and savor your answers. On your marks, get set, let's go!

One thing I know for sure: you are a gift to someone (and, more than likely, a lot of people). You are unique and have gifts that no other person on earth has. It is very important that you take the time to recognize what your unique qualities are. You are meant to shine in a different way than everyone else.

What is one thing that is truly unique about you, and how is it a gift to others?

Learning about your heritage, celebrating family traditions, embracing your culture, and having an appreciation for where you came from can open your eyes to how beautiful and unique you are.

What is one thing about your family history that you are very proud of?

Living with anticipation is good for the soul. When you anticipate upcoming fun, it improves your mood.

What is something fun you are looking forward to doing with your friends or family?

It doesn't have to change the world for you to consider it an achievement. It is important that you take the time to be proud of yourself when you accomplish small and large goals.

What is a recent achievement you're proud of?

It has been said that a picture is worth a thousand words.

What is an example of a picture that tells a beautiful story? Describe what the picture is and the story it tells.

"Sometimes you will never know the true value of a moment until it becomes a memory."

-Dr. Seuss

When you were a child and would race out the door on a Saturday morning during the summer, where would you spend most of your time? What is your best memory from that place?

Never underestimate the value of your hard work. When you accomplish something because you worked hard, it is so rewarding, as well as a reminder of what you can achieve when you work hard.

What in your life have you worked the hardest at, and what were the results?

_____

_____

_____

_____

_____

_____

_____

_____

_____

_____

_____

_____

When you know what you want your legacy to be, you can start building it. It will be the guide to live your life in the way you want to be remembered.

What do you want your legacy to be?

_____

_____

_____

_____

_____

_____

_____

_____

_____

_____

_____

_____

When was a time you were braver than you ever though you could be, and what were the results of your bravery?

Self-discipline is an essential skill in every area of our lives. It gives us the necessary willpower required to do what needs to be done.

In what area of your life do you exercise the most self-discipline, and when was the last time it really came into play?

_____

_____

_____

_____

_____

_____

_____

_____

_____

_____

_____

_____

Faith in God requires complete trust. Sometimes our prayers are answered right away, or it may take days, weeks, months, or even years. When a prayer is answered, most describe it as a memory they will never forget.

What is the biggest prayer you have ever had answered?

The expression "my cup of tea" has been around since the late 1800s. It describes something you like, enjoy, or are good at.

What is your "cup of tea," and why?

A hero represents the process of overcoming obstacles to achieve great things. Heroes elevate us emotionally and encourage us to change our lives for the better and to help others.

Who are the heroes in your life, and why?

_____

_____

_____

_____

_____

_____

_____

_____

_____

_____

_____

"Where there is a human being, there is an opportunity for kindness."

-Lucius Annaeus Seneca

You deserve kindness. Everyone does, but for many different reasons.

Why do you deserve kindness?

_____

_____

_____

_____

_____

_____

_____

_____

_____

_____

_____

_____

_____

_____

Songwriters have an amazing way of telling emotional stories that we can relate to.

What song touches you emotionally, and why?

_____

_____

_____

_____

_____

_____

_____

_____

_____

_____

_____

_____

There are so many people who take someone or something for granted. Often they don't even realize they are doing it until it is too late. They just expect that someone or something to always be available.

What is one thing most people take for granted that you never will, and why do you feel that way?

Our childhood home is almost always a treasure trove of memories.

What is your fondest memory within the house you grew up in?

Are there things in your life that are important enough to make them a personal commandment?

What are three personal commandments you want to live by?

_____

_____

_____

_____

_____

_____

_____

_____

_____

_____

_____

_____

_____

_____

One of the most difficult compliments to give is to yourself. Few things build self-confidence faster than your ability to recognize and appreciate your own qualities.

What is something you love about yourself?

Being an inspiration to someone means you help them see an even higher level of achievement than they see on their own. You are able to propel them over limitations that might be holding them back.

Who do you inspire, and how?

When was a memorable time that you laughed—like, really laughed—and could not stop even when you tried? What is the story behind it?

_____

_____

_____

_____

_____

_____

_____

_____

_____

_____

_____

_____

_____

_____

It's the little things that make us happy, most often. The little things are the most accessible and frequent; they are the ones that save the day.

What little things make you happy?

Travel has proven to improve people's mental and physical health. Travel is an excellent way to learn more about yourself while you are out of your comfort zone.

Where do you want to visit in the next year, and why?

One great thing about lifelong learning and experience is that they change us over time. That change allows us to embrace new things in our life that we wouldn't have otherwise.

How have you changed over the last five years?

When things seem a little rough in the world, hope allows us to look ahead with optimism. Hope is the belief that things will get better.

What is something in the news today that gives you hope, and why?

_____

_____

_____

_____

_____

_____

_____

_____

_____

_____

_____

_____

_____

Summer is the time of vacations, barbecues on the grill, and hanging out at the pool or beach. Summer also provides significant benefits to our health and wellbeing.

Sunlight helps regulate almost all of our bodily processes as well as creates an environment that improves our lifestyle.

What are three things you like to do during the summer, and why?

_____

_____

_____

_____

_____

_____

_____

_____

_____

_____

_____

_____

Don't let your past hold you back from setting big goals. You must live with anticipation to achieve big things.

What are three big goals you have for yourself?

When you are confident in your beliefs, you are able to stave off doing something you will regret for short-term gain.

What are three things you are not willing to sacrifice for professional success, and why?

Taking the time to acknowledge and record small daily accomplishments, no matter how small, is so important. The feeling of accomplishment makes us happy and satisfied. Taking the time to savor that feeling will help inspire you to seek that feeling again.

What is one thing you accomplished today?

As we travel through life, we all pick up traits that will stay with us for the rest of our lives.

What are the three important traits you want to instill in your children or other young people?

_____

_____

_____

_____

_____

_____

_____

_____

_____

_____

_____

_____

Very rarely do we make it to where we want to be without the help of others.

Who are three people who have helped you get to where you are professionally, and what did they do to help?

There is something inside that is calling on you to create. Not something for your job, but something for you. Maybe a garden, a piece of art, or a project that gives you a sense of purpose. Having something to dive into when you need a positive direction will improve your quality of life.

What do you really want to create?

There is a common belief that everyone is motivated by a fear or a reward.

What reward motivates you the most, and why?

_____

_____

_____

_____

_____

_____

_____

_____

_____

_____

_____

_____

_____

What is it that truly touches you deep in your soul? Is it the thrill of victory, something you created with your own hands, looking at pictures of the places you want to visit someday, or standing out in nature and taking in all its beauty?

What is it that touches you like that, and why?

What do you value? If your life were to change drastically—say you became world famous, or you lost everything—what values would be unaffected?

What three important values are you not willing to compromise?

_____

_____

_____

_____

_____

_____

_____

_____

_____

_____

_____

_____

_____

It takes a very special person to give you honest feedback. Sometimes even our closest friends can't bring themselves to deliver the hard or bad news.

Who is that one person you can count on for honest feedback, and when was the last time they gave it to you?

We have all had to do it. It often comes when we have no other choice.

When was the last time you had to stand up for yourself, and how did it make you stronger?

_____

_____

_____

_____

_____

_____

_____

_____

_____

_____

_____

We grow through the process of taking risks. Whether it works out or not, we can gain confidence, which in turn helps us take more risks that will improve our chances of success.

What is the biggest risk you have ever taken that was so worth it in the end?

Receiving an unexpected gift can be a huge mood changer. It makes you feel loved, appreciated, and valued.

What was the last unexpected gift you received that really made you feel good, and what was special about it?

_____

_____

_____

_____

_____

_____

_____

_____

_____

_____

_____

_____

_____

"Family is free and priceless all at the same time."

-Mike Parker

Think of your family, what it stands for, and what it means to you. Family is often the place we return to for comfort, love, and support.

What is the best thing about being part of your family?

Sacrifice is rarely fun. It means you are giving up one thing for something you feel is more important or valuable.

What is the biggest sacrifice you have made in your life, and why?

We all have topics we would prefer to avoid and topics we could go on all day about.

What are your three favorite topics to talk about, and why?

_____

_____

_____

_____

_____

_____

_____

_____

_____

_____

_____

_____

_____

_____

_____

How would you finish this sentence:
"My proudest moment in life so
far is . . ."?

It is so important to be able to consciously add value to someone's life. Your kind words, support, encouragement, and even gifts can have a lasting impact on someone's life.

Who are three people that truly add value to your life, and how does each one add value?

When we hear good news, it increases our happiness and life satisfaction. It gives us a positive way forward.

What is the best news you have received lately?

"And now these three remain: faith, hope and love. But the greatest of these is love."

–Paul the Apostle, 1 Corinthians 13:13 (NIV)

The power in these three simple words can be life changing. Whether it's the first time or the most recent time, they can stop us in our tracks.

Who was the last person to say "I love you" to you, and what were the circumstances that led to it?

Scientific evidence suggests that being happy may have major benefits for your health. Happiness can boost your immune system, protect your heart, reduce pain, and even improve your life expectancy. You benefit from being mindful of what makes you happy.

What are three things that make you happy?

In this fast-paced world we live in, sometimes we don't slow down enough to make sure those around us know how much we care about them.

With whom has it been too long since you shared how much they mean to you? What would you want to say to them?

No matter your age, continuing to learn is so important to growing as a person.

What is the most recent thing you have learned to do?

Having fun should be taken much more seriously. Doing things that are fun have so many health benefits, from balancing out stress, improving our energy, fighting off depression, and even preventing disease. It is also good for our mind to think about past activities that were fun.

What was the last really fun thing you did?

What was your favorite family activity when you were growing up, and what do you remember most about it?

_____

_____

_____

_____

_____

_____

_____

_____

_____

_____

_____

_____

Here is how powerful a compliment is: several studies have shown that receiving a compliment has the same effect as receiving cash.

Who was the last person you paid a compliment to, and what was it for?

Professional goals might include advancing up the corporate ladder, starting a new business, changing careers, or going back to school. They help motivate you to strive toward a new target and reach a new level of success.

What is your biggest professional goal for the next year?

_____

_____

_____

_____

_____

_____

_____

_____

_____

_____

_____

_____

Having a positive influence on someone's life is important to everyone's personal and professional development. If someone has a positive influence on your life, they have made an emotional connection with you that has led to you having a high level of trust in their ideas and opinions.

Who are the three biggest influences in your life, and how do they influence you?

There is so much tradition found in the kitchen.

What meal did your mom or dad teach you to cook that you want to pass down to your children?

Passing on what you have learned during your life journey is how you can best help the next generation.

If you could give a child three pieces of advice, what would they be?

_____

_____

_____

_____

_____

_____

_____

_____

_____

_____

_____

_____

_____

_____

Honesty is about so much more than just telling the truth. It's about being real with who you are and what you feel. True authenticity can only be shared with someone in whom you have the highest level of trust.

Who is that one person you can be completely honest with, and why them?

Goals are a great way to focus on where you want to get to, and they give you something to look forward to. Goals become much more useful when you are mindful of the rewards that will come along with achieving them. They create an extra level of motivation.

What is one goal you have for this year, and what rewards will come with reaching your goal?

Happiness is something nearly everyone strives for. It is so powerful, it has even been shown to affect how long we live. When things are far from perfect and your life is starting to weigh on you, it's important to be mindful of something that can change your focus and mood.

What is one thing you can count on to always make you happy?

We spend more time alone than with people. Often when we are alone, we use our thoughts to keep us company. Being able to focus on positive thoughts while we are alone has a major impact on our well-being.

What is your favorite thing to think about when you are alone, and why?

Passion is a powerful force. You can be passionate about something simple or something life changing; it doesn't matter so long as passion is flowing through your body and mind.

What is the one thing in your life that you are the most passionate about, and why?

_____

_____

_____

_____

_____

_____

_____

_____

_____

_____

_____

_____

_____

Knowing someone believes in you is powerful and uplifting. It can be so encouraging, it can feel like a superpower.

Who are three people who believe in you, and how have they shown that belief in you?

What would you say is your most cherished family keepsake or heirloom, and why?

"Gratitude helps you fall in love with the life you already have."

-Kristen Hewitt

As a reminder for when you need it, make two ongoing lists that you add to over time. They will be your Grateful Lists.

What are the big things and what are the small things you are grateful for in your life?

_____

_____

_____

_____

_____

_____

_____

_____

_____

_____

_____

_____

If you have lived, you have learned. Your life experience is one of the most valuable assets you have. Your willingness to share what you have learned is one thing that will help the next generation prosper.

What are three things you have learned in life that you want others to know?

_____

_____

_____

_____

_____

_____

_____

_____

_____

_____

_____

_____

_____

We live with hopeful expectation that the next big opportunity will come our way. It would be silly to have that expectation and not be ready.

What is the next big opportunity in your life that you want to make sure you are ready for?

Having good friends is important, but having people in your life you can count on is even more valuable.

Who is one person you can talk to when you need a pick-me-up, and when was the last time they came through for you?

_____

_____

_____

_____

_____

_____

_____

_____

_____

_____

_____

Life is better with friends. The best way to assure you have great friends is to be a great friend.

What makes you a great friend?

Who is the one person you rarely see that you wish would surprise you by walking in the door? What would you be excited to tell them?

_____

_____

_____

_____

_____

_____

_____

_____

_____

_____

_____

_____

_____

Believe it or not, food has a huge impact on your state of mind. Home-cooked meals often have tradition and history attached to them. Our favorite foods often not only satisfy our hunger, but also make us happy.

What is your favorite home-cooked meal that you make? Describe the history or tradition that comes with it.

_____

_____

_____

_____

_____

_____

_____

_____

_____

_____

_____

_____

When life gets a little tough, it's important to do something to lift your spirits. Something as simple as opening the blinds, going for a walk, or buying some flowers can do the trick. It is also helpful to have somewhere you can go, someplace that you know will lift your spirits.

Where can you go to lift your spirits, and what is special about this place?

A good song can change our mood in just a few notes. It can get you up and moving and have such a positive effect on our emotions.

What song brings a smile to your face, and why?

Nearly everyone has been able to gather knowledge over their lifetime in one thing or another.

What is a topic you are very knowledgeable about, and what led to that knowledge?

Grandparents are such a valuable resource, full of wisdom, experiences, heritage, and family history. They are often able to connect children to the past better than anyone.

What is one thing your grandparents have taught you?

Loneliness can affect anyone at any time. It can come on when you are in a room of people or when you are totally by yourself. Having someone to turn to is a powerful defense against loneliness.

When you feel lonely, who is the person you can most count on to help, and why do you feel they are best for this role?

_____

_____

_____

_____

_____

_____

_____

_____

_____

_____

_____

There are few things more exhilarating and memorable than trying new experiences.

What is the last "new thing" you tried that ended up being way better than you thought it would be? How so?

_____

_____

_____

_____

_____

_____

_____

_____

_____

_____

_____

_____

When you close your eyes in the shade on a lazy summer Saturday afternoon and let your mind wander, where do your thoughts most often go, and why?

"Fear is a reaction.
Courage is a decision."

-Winston Churchill

There is a song entitled "Fear is a Liar" by Zach Williams. In almost every case, the fear you have never materializes or is way overblown.

When was a time that your courage allowed you to overcome fear?

Often, money helps make our lives more manageable and comfortable. Though it is important, it should never be the most important thing in our lives.

What are three things more important ant to you than money, and why?

_____

_____

_____

_____

_____

_____

_____

_____

_____

_____

_____

_____

_____

What was the best thing about the past weekend that you would like to remember?

_____

_____

_____

_____

_____

_____

_____

_____

_____

_____

_____

_____

_____

Second-guessing yourself often leads to indecision. Believing that you are more than capable of making the right decision sometimes comes very slowly.

What is one decision you have been putting off that needs to be made?

_____

_____

_____

_____

_____

_____

_____

_____

_____

_____

_____

_____

_____

_____

Being proud of yourself is something most people really struggle to acknowledge.

What is the last thing you did that you are really proud of?

Never underestimate the power of even the smallest victories. They create some of the best memories and shared stories of our lives.

What was your favorite victory from your high school days?

A university report showed that having a friend over a long period can add years to your life. A friend you have known for many years tends to be more understanding and flexible, which leads to a happier and healthier friendship.

Who is your most long-standing friend to this day, and why has your friendship lasted so long?

Short-term goals are the most effective way to zero in on your next achievement.

What is one short-term goal for this week?

Everyone has their own strengths and weaknesses. Most people have no trouble listing their weaknesses, so we will leave that for another day.

What are your strengths—all of them?

_____

_____

_____

_____

_____

_____

_____

_____

_____

_____

_____

_____

A bucket list is a great way to keep track of and work toward your dream experiences. When you are able to cross something off your bucket list, it should create a lasting memory.

What is the biggest thing you have done off your bucket list, and what are your best memories from that experience?

Smiling has been shown to lower our heart rate and blood pressure. Smiling not only improves your personal health and well-being, but also has a huge positive impact on those around you.

Who are three people you can count on to put a smile on your face, and why are they good at it?

"We dont remember days, we remember moments."

-Cesare Pavese

What is your best memory from being a member of a team?

Most people say that if their house were on fire, the first material thing they would grab are their photos.

Whether they are in a box, an album, or on your phone, which old picture sends you down memory lane the most? Describe what you see in that picture that makes it so special.

_____

_____

_____

_____

_____

_____

_____

_____

_____

_____

_____

_____

There are a lot of great ideas for new businesses that never get off the ground because most people don't have access to the money it takes to start them.

If you had the money, what business would you love to start, and why would it be a success with you at the top?

Life is made up of constant decisions. No matter who you are or where you find yourself on the food chain, you have to make decisions every day.

Everyone has made good ones that have worked out even better than they thought and others that didn't work out at all.

What is the best decision you have made so far in your life, and why do you think it was?

_____

_____

_____

_____

_____

_____

_____

_____

_____

_____

_____

There is something heartfelt about taking the time to write down your kind thoughts about someone, something that just isn't felt in an email or text message.

To whom do you need to write a thank-you note, and why?

_____

_____

_____

_____

_____

_____

_____

_____

_____

_____

_____

Being dependable shows others that you care, you respect them, and they are important. When you are viewed as dependable, it helps foster trust.

Who would you say depends on you the most, and why?

Passing down family stories helps the next generation connect with its past. Researchers report that children who are informed about their family history have high self-esteem and are better able to form an identity with their past.

What is one beautiful story from your life you plan to tell your children and grandchildren, and why?

_____

_____

_____

_____

_____

_____

_____

_____

_____

_____

_____

Inner peace helps calm our mind and allows you to enjoy life on a deeper, more satisfying level.

What gives you the most inner peace?

Memories of your most rewarding experiences have the most lasting impact.

What has been the most rewarding experience of your life so far, and why?

_____

_____

_____

_____

_____

_____

_____

_____

_____

_____

_____

_____

_____

There is no doubt that beauty is in the eyes of the beholder. Some might find beauty in a glorious sunset, while others might find it in fascinating, snow-covered trees.

What are three things you would say are beautiful, and how does each one make you feel?

When we have a sense of security, we feel empowered, comfortable, and safe. It is important to be mindful of what makes us feel secure.

What gives you a sense of security, and why?

We don't need research to show us that doing something kind for someone makes us and the recipient feel good. Selfless acts done for no reason other than to make someone feel happier are so special, and they in turn make the recipient more likely to be kind to the next person.

What is the greatest act of kindness you have ever done for someone?

What is one thing you are a "natural" at, and how did you discover this talent?

The world is full of astonishing, fascinating, and sacred things to see and experience—things that take our breath away and touch us in a deep way.

What in this world are you in awe of?

_____

_____

_____

_____

_____

_____

_____

_____

_____

_____

_____

_____

What is something simple that brings you joy?

No matter our age, sometimes we all need a little nudge to get going. Often, we know what needs to be done but are hesitant to do it.

Who is the person that best gets you going, and when was a time they did so?

_____

_____

_____

_____

_____

_____

_____

_____

_____

_____

_____

_____

_____

"I love when someone's laugh is funnier than the joke."

—Anonymous

Laughter triggers the release of endorphins, the body's natural feel-good chemicals. Laughter is so powerful, it actually causes a physical change in your body.

What made you laugh today?

_____

_____

_____

_____

_____

_____

_____

_____

_____

_____

_____

_____

_____

_____

_____

_____

Getting a gift feels wonderful. Besides the gift itself, receiving it creates a lasting memory.

What is the best gift you have ever received, and why? Who gave it to you?

Purpose can guide your decision making, affect your be-
havior, guide your goals, and bring meaning to your life.

What do you see as your purpose in life?

_____

_____

_____

_____

_____

_____

_____

_____

_____

_____

_____

_____

_____

We all keep some things about who and what we are about to ourselves.

What is one fact about you that most people don't know?

Life can be like a roller coaster. We go through periods where everything seems in doubt, and other times when we feel self-assured.

In what area of your life are you feeling the most self-assured right now, and why?

_____

_____

_____

_____

_____

_____

_____

_____

_____

_____

_____

_____

There are a lot of different emotions: some positive, some not.

Which of the positive emotions (joy, surprise, trust, anticipation, excitement, or another) do you display the most, and why?

Generosity is a quality found in those who are happy to give to others. The Bible says in the book of Proverbs that a generous person will prosper; whoever refreshes others will be refreshed. Your generosity helps build confidence and strengthens your well-being.

What has been the most generous act of your life so far?

_____

_____

_____

_____

_____

_____

_____

_____

_____

_____

_____

_____

A friend needs your advice on how to get through a difficult time.

What would you want them to know? What unique message, words of wisdom, or encouragement would be your personal message to them?

_____

_____

_____

_____

_____

_____

_____

_____

_____

_____

_____

_____

How many times have you asked, "Why didn't I think of that?" What has been your all-time brightest idea?

_____

_____

_____

_____

_____

_____

_____

_____

_____

_____

_____

_____

_____

You're the coach (pick any sport) and your team needs an inspiring short speech right before the competition begins. The success of your team hangs on your every word.

What would you tell them?

"Stop worrying about what might be around the corner and start enjoying where you are today."

–Mike Parker

Celebrations make life more enjoyable and fun. They also create some awesome memories.

In your life, what has been your biggest reason to celebrate?

Choose a person close to you and identify something about them that makes them special.

When was the last time you told them they were special, and what was it you shared?

The lessons we learn and the strength we gain during our setbacks can be what leads to future successes.

What was your biggest setback, and how did you overcome it?

_____

_____

_____

_____

_____

_____

_____

_____

_____

_____

_____

_____

_____

_____

What are three material things you have that you would describe as irreplaceable, and why?

"I love people who can make me laugh when I dont even want to smile."

—Anonymous

Knowing who the people are that make you laugh is one of the most valuable lists you can have. Laughter provides us with so many health benefits—we should always be looking for opportunities for humor and laughter.

Who makes you laugh without even trying, and how do they do it?

You are interviewing someone to be your personal assistant.

What are the three qualities they would need to have to get the job, and why?

There is mounting research that shows there are psychological benefits to being grateful, such as being happier and feeling less stress. Feeling grateful allows you to truly appreciate what you have right now.

What are the three things you are the most grateful for right now, and why?

Today is a day full of relaxation with yourself.

What specific things will you do to relax (morning, afternoon, and night) for a full day?

_____

_____

_____

_____

_____

_____

_____

_____

_____

_____

_____

_____

_____

Validation is when you feel heard and understood. It's when others acknowledge and accept the way you feel, even if they don't totally agree with you.

When was a time you felt completely validated?

To grow is to change and develop over time. Every day we have the opportunity to grow in maturity, knowledge, success, and happiness.

Due to your personal growth, what is one thing you can do today that you could not do last year?

_____

_____

_____

_____

_____

_____

_____

_____

_____

_____

_____

We often feel so paralyzed by the fear that we will make the wrong decision that we make no decision at all.

What is something you know would change your life for the better, but that you can't bring yourself to do?

_____

_____

_____

_____

_____

_____

_____

_____

_____

_____

_____

_____

_____

The impact of any one piece of gratitude is small, but the cumulative effect is monumental.

What are three things from today that you are grateful for, and why?

_____

_____

_____

_____

_____

_____

_____

_____

_____

_____

_____

_____

_____

_____

"The giving of love is an education in itself."

–Eleanor Roosevelt

Being there for someone who needs you is often never for-gotten. The security and comfort it can bring someone can be lifesaving.

When was a time someone really needed you and you came through for them?

Lifelong learning will help you adapt to an ever-changing world. When you stop learning, you stop growing.

What is the most valuable thing you have learned this year?

There are some things that no one can do for you as well as you can do for yourself.

What would you do today, if you could do anything, for yourself?

_____

_____

_____

_____

_____

_____

_____

_____

_____

_____

_____

_____

_____

_____

_____

Being relaxed has many health benefits, such as helping your immune and cardiovascular systems work at their optimal level.

What activity relaxes you, and why?

_____

_____

_____

_____

_____

_____

_____

_____

_____

_____

_____

_____

_____

_____

_____

Other than your parents or grandparents, who has taught you the best life lesson of your life so far, and what is it?

"Memories are perhaps
the best gifts of all."

–Gloria Gaither

Music makes us feel nostalgic and has an incredible impact on our thoughts. Just a couple of seconds into a song can take your thoughts miles or years away.

What song best takes you back to a childhood memory, and what is that memory?

_____

_____

_____

_____

_____

_____

_____

_____

_____

_____

_____

_____

_____

It's never too early or too late when it comes to learning.

What is something you want to learn in the next year?

Make sure you always have that one comfort food on hand, the one that not only tastes good in your mouth, but also comforts your entire body.

What is your go-to comfort food, and why?

Volunteering can be a long-term, life-changing event. It says a lot about who you are and what you care about.

What is one organization you would like to volunteer with, and why?

_____

_____

_____

_____

_____

_____

_____

_____

_____

_____

_____

_____

"Happiness is like a kiss. You must share it to enjoy it."

-Bernard Meltzer

Happiness is a skill that can be learned.

How do you use your skills to make others happy?

_____

_____

_____

_____

_____

_____

_____

_____

_____

_____

_____

_____

_____

_____

A publishing company has offered you a large amount of money for the rights to your autobiography.

What would the title be, and what area of your life would you write the most about? Why?

Who was the last person that made you feel truly appreciated, and what do you remember most about that situation?

Every parent wants to teach their children to be respectful, thankful, and honest. Beyond the typical lessons, most parents have their own individual belief or some indispensable life lessons they want to instill in their children.

What is the most important thing your parents instilled in you?

We tend to focus on our biggest accomplishments; yet nearly every day, we have very meaningful and inspiring accomplishments that we just plow right through.

Most are not life altering, but are still important and can be a source of pride when we take the time to reflect on them.

What did you accomplish today?

"Life is either a daring adventure or nothing at all."

-Helen Keller

Everyone's life journey has taught them valuable lessons that only life can teach.

What is the most important lesson life has taught you that you would like the next generation to learn, and why?

You have skills, and everyone knows it.

What is one thing people are always asking you to help them with, and when was the last situation in which you got asked?

Being able to provide good advice is a very important social skill.

What is the best advice you have ever given someone?

If you only knew then what you know now.

What moment in your past would you enjoy reliving, and why?

_____

_____

_____

_____

_____

_____

_____

_____

_____

_____

_____

_____

_____

When you pay it forward, you are willingly impacting someone's life for the better.

Have you ever paid it forward? If so, what did you do?

_____

_____

_____

_____

_____

_____

_____

_____

_____

_____

_____

_____

_____

_____

_____

Enthusiasm is being excited and having a keen interest in something.

What was the last thing you were enthusiastic about, and why?

_____

_____

_____

_____

_____

_____

_____

_____

_____

_____

_____

_____

_____

"Success is not found in yesterday's achievements but in today's effort."

-Mike Parker

Effort is one thing that everyone respects. It says you care and that something is important to you.

What is one thing you consistently give your greatest effort to?

We all have things in our life we want to outlive us.

What is something you want to archive from your life, and why?

_____

_____

_____

_____

_____

_____

_____

_____

_____

_____

_____

_____

_____

Inspiration is the force that makes you want to be motivated. When someone is able to inspire you, they instill a wave of both mental and physical energy that helps propel you to your full potential.

Who is the person that inspires you, and how do they do it?

_____

_____

_____

_____

_____

_____

_____

_____

_____

_____

_____

_____

_____

_____

As years go by, our earliest memories can change. There is something precious about our childhood memories.

What is the earliest memory you have that you cherish?

_____

_____

_____

_____

_____

_____

_____

_____

_____

_____

_____

_____

Many of the greatest stories of humanity are comeback stories. Everyone loves a great comeback story. When you reflect back on your own, I bet it strikes up feelings of great pride.

What has been your greatest comeback?

"We can't help everyone, but everyone can help someone."

-Ronald Reagan

Helping others brings a deeper level of meaningfulness to our lives. We all have had times in our life when someone unexpectedly helped us, and these moments often create memories we are grateful to have.

Who could you help tomorrow, and how?

The benefits of being part of a team goes far beyond winning the championship, a gold medal, or acquiring a skill.

What was the best lesson you learned from being a part of a team?

We all love to hear a compliment. It doesn't matter if it comes from someone you have known your whole life or from someone you just met today.

Who is someone you can compliment tomorrow? Why did you pick this person?

_____

_____

_____

_____

_____

_____

_____

_____

_____

_____

_____

_____

_____

Everyone has that one person they love to hear from. When your phone says you have a text message, or when you're at work and see you have an email, you get a little extra excitement when you see it's from them.

Who is the one person you love to hear from, and why?

_____

_____

_____

_____

_____

_____

_____

_____

_____

_____

_____

_____

Every day we make thousands of choices.

If you were to make a better choice than the one you made the first time, what choice would it be?

_____

_____

_____

_____

_____

_____

_____

_____

_____

_____

_____

_____

You need advice—whom do you ask, and why?

_____

_____

_____

_____

_____

_____

_____

_____

_____

_____

_____

_____

_____

_____

Making someone smile is one of the most gracious things you can do. Smiling is so powerful, even therapists recommend it as part of therapy.

Who do you want to make smile tomorrow, and why?

You are a guest speaker at an elementary school, and you will be talking to a classroom of first-grade students.

What do you want them to know?

If you had to pick one thing from your childhood that you are proudest of, what would you pick, and why?

_____

_____

_____

_____

_____

_____

_____

_____

_____

_____

_____

_____

We have all been there: we know it's time to take that next big step in our life, but the fear of the unknown holds us back. But ignoring it could be worse than taking it and failing.

What is the next big step in your life, and why do you think you will be ready for it?

_____

_____

_____

_____

_____

_____

_____

_____

_____

_____

_____

_____

Almost every family has a black sheep or colorful character in it.

What's the best memory you have about one of your family's black sheep?

Research has shown that nature is crucial to our mental and physical well-being. Going on a walk is a great way to clear our mind. Go back to your best outside walk.

Where was it, and what do you remember the most about it?

Our greatest memories are often with our family. The memories that are told from a parent's perspective, and later from the child's perspective, are priceless.

What is the next big thing you want to do with your kids (or parents, or both) that will create one of these memories?

Developing a positive self-image is so important to our mental health. When you treat yourself with compassion, you will be able to acknowledge your strengths and accept your flaws.

What do you like when you look in the mirror?

Visualization is one of our minds' most powerful tools. It can take you anywhere in the world you want to be.

When you visualize the perfect "room with a view," where is it and what do you see?

Many people won't try something new unless they know it will be a success. Don't let fear call the shots.

What is something you are afraid to try but really want to?

We need someone to look up to, no matter our age. Having someone that we respect and admire helps us strive to become a better person.

Whom do you most look up to, and why?

What has been the single most satisfying moment of your life so far?

Research shows that receiving a compliment can improve our relationships and general happiness.

Who was the last person to pay you a compliment, and what was it for?

Having a long-term goal in your profession is a great driving force behind continuing to learn and grow.

Where do you want to be professionally when you retire?

Family traditions mean so much more than just something you do together. They carry with them so many stories of times gone by.

What is your best memory of a family tradition?

_____

_____

_____

_____

_____

_____

_____

_____

_____

_____

_____

_____

_____

_____

Don't let the speed of life stop you from taking the time to savor small victories, accomplishments, and fun times.

What was the best part of your week?

Above all else, passion is a feeling. Being passionate boils down to feeling really strongly about something.

What are three things you are very passionate about, and why?

When you feel empowered, you don't seek validation from others. Instead, your knowledge, confidence, and ability allow you to make decisions for yourself.

What is one thing that empowers you, and why?

What are you the most optimistic
about in your life right now, and why?

Who is your favorite person to share a meal with, and what is it about them that makes it so special?

Gaining new knowledge and advancing yourself as an individual makes you feel accomplished.

What has been a new moment of growth in your life?

Today is the day. After years of work and a lifetime of memories, it's your last day at your workplace.

What do you want your coworkers to highlight at your retirement party?

Self-discovery allows you to put all the pieces of the life puzzle together. You will have a deeper understanding of what you want, enjoy, and cherish the most. It will bring you closer to those you love, appreciate, and value.

After answering the questions within this book, what has been your greatest self-discovery?

References

"Dr. Seuss Quotes (Images)." QuotesWave. Accessed September 23, 2021. https://www.quoteswave.com/picture-quotes/62998.

"Lucius Annaeus Seneca Quotes." BrainyQuote. Accessed September 23, 2021. https://www.brainyquote.com/quotes/lucius_annaeus_seneca_106288.

Kristen Hewitt, "33 Simple Ways to Create a Happier and Healthier Life Right Now," *Kristen Hewitt* (blog), https://kristenhewitt.me/33-simple-ways-to-create-a-happier-and-healthier-life-right-now/.

Winston Churchill, PassItOn. Accessed September 23, 2021. https://www.passiton.com/inspirational-quotes/7517-fear-is-a-reaction-courage-is-a-decision.

Pavese, Cesare. *The Burning Brand: Diaries 1935-1950*. Walker, 1961.

Loveforquotes.com. Accessed September 23, 2021. Loveforquotes.com/i/2956209.

Yoddler. Accessed September 23, 2021. Yoddler.com/?page=/Quote&q=286#page=/Quote&q=286.

Eleanor Roosevelt, "Best Love Quotes and Sayings in 2021." QuoteStudy. Accessed September 23, 2021. Quotestudy.xyz/love-quotes-sayings/.

"Gloria Gaither Quotes." AZquotes. Accessed September 23, 2021. Azquotes.com/author/25178-Gloris-Gaither.

Bernard Meltzer, "Quotations on Happiness." Optimanage. com. Accessed September 23, 2021. Optimanage.com/quotations8.html.

Keller, Hellen. *Let Us Have Faith*. Doubleday, Doran & Co., Inc., 1940.

"Ronald Reagan Quotes." BrainyQuote. Accessed September 23, 2021. Brainyquotes.com/quotes/ronald_reagan-120491.

About The Author

Mike Parker has been delivering motivational presentations for over twenty years. He is driven by his passion to help others achieve more than they ever thought was possible by igniting their full potential. Mike has a clear and inspiring message about the qualities found in overachieving people, teams, and organizations. Mike has been able to inspire thousands of individuals through his motivational presentations and his work as a Success Coach.

As a former track and field athlete at the University of Kansas, and now as a coach who built one of the country's most successful programs, he has firsthand knowledge of what it takes to get to the top and enjoy the journey along the way. His girls cross country and track and field teams at Iowa City West High School have won eleven Class 4A team state titles.

Mike's firsthand knowledge of how to ignite individual and team peak performances has helped thousands of individuals and many teams, organizations, and corporations reach amazing success. Due to the success of his teams, Mike has been selected as the Iowa High School

State Coach of the Year or the At-Large Coach of the Year thirty-two times. Mike has been a finalist for National Coach of the Year awards three different times. In 2018, the National High School Athletic Coaches Association selected Mike as the Girls Track and Field National Coach of the Year, and in 2022 they inducted Mike into the National High School Athletic Coaches Association Hall of Fame.

Mike is a sought-after keynote speaker by major corporations, associations, colleges, and school districts, and his strategies and ideas on how to use Your Best Effort Every Time, Compassion as a Leadership Skill, and Ask Yourself for Health, Happiness and Self-Discovery have helped turn around underperforming teams, transformed organizations and ignited the full potential in thousands of individuals.

For more information on Mike's work and his keynotes, seminars, professional development, and other inspiring services, visit him online:

askyourselfbook.com

mike-parker.com

 MotivationalSpeakerMikeParker

askyourselfbook